Thank you for your purchase!

Useful Tip!
If you prefer coloring with markers, it's recommended that you place a blank sheet of paper behind the page to prevent any bleed–through.

HAPPY COLORING!

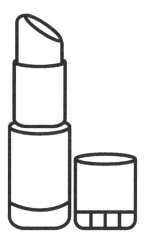

COLOR TEST PAGE

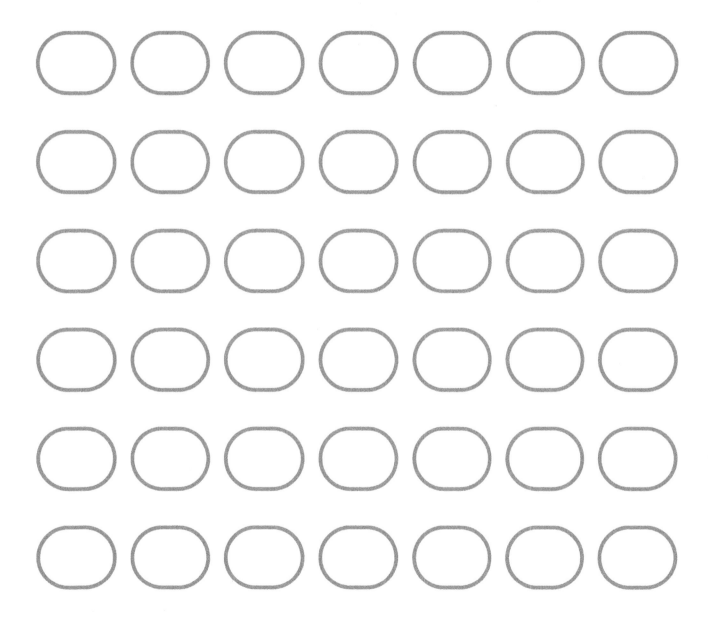

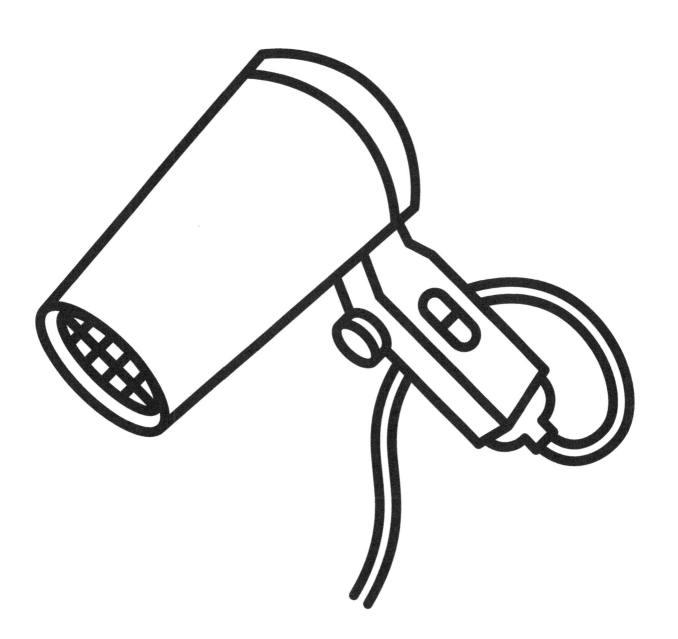

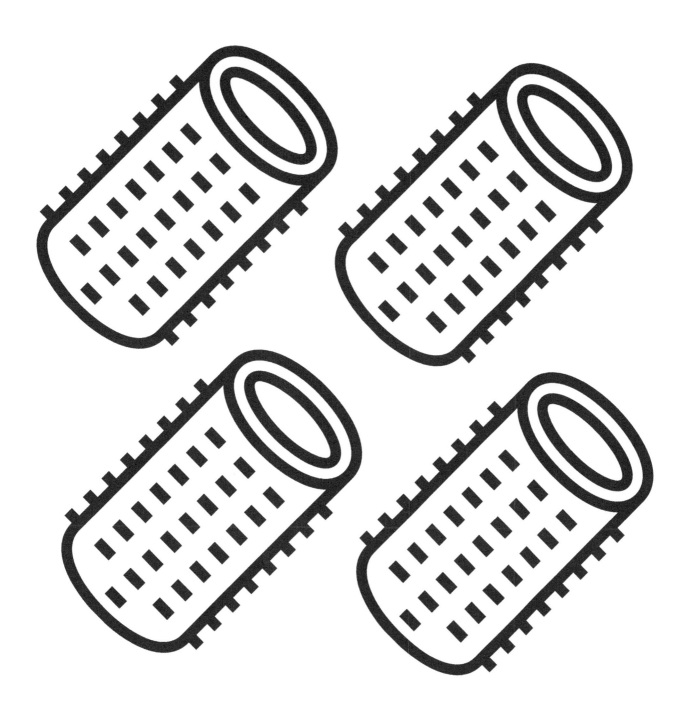

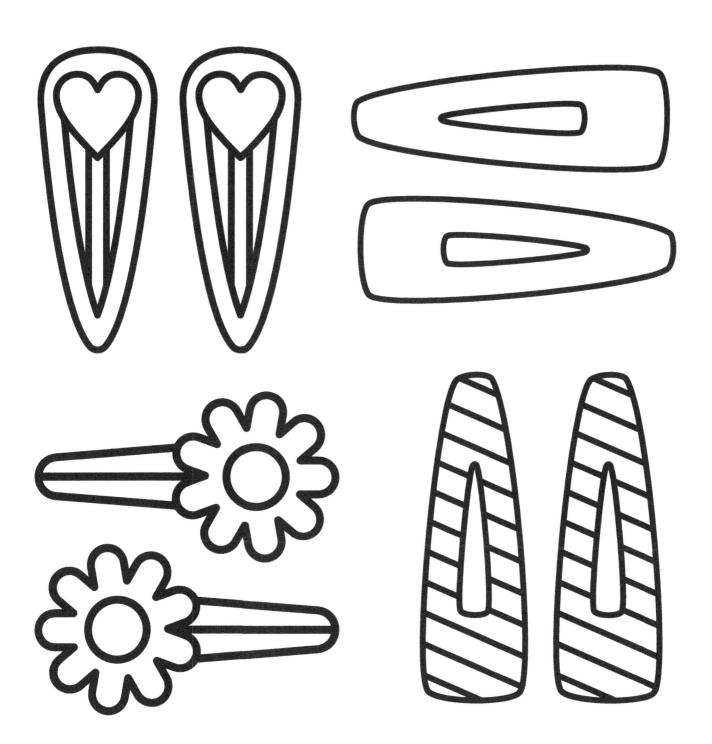

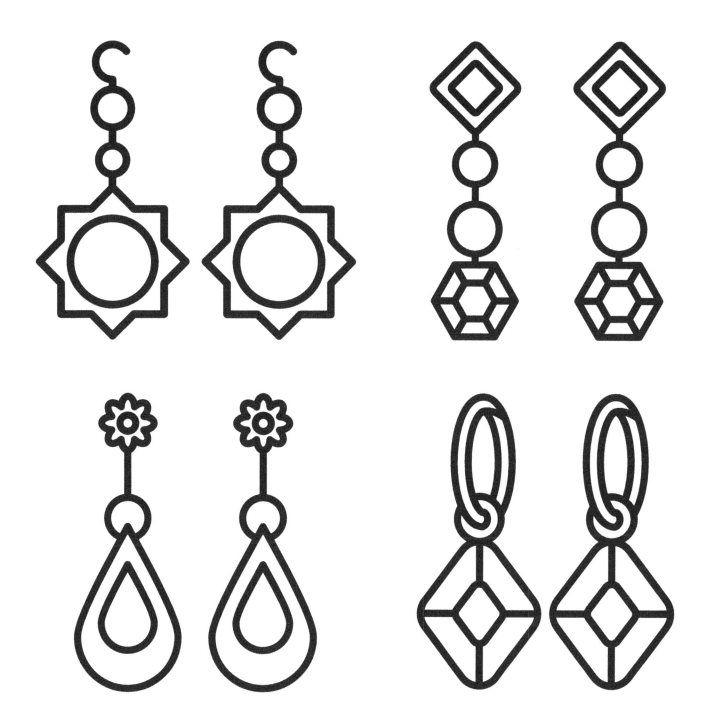

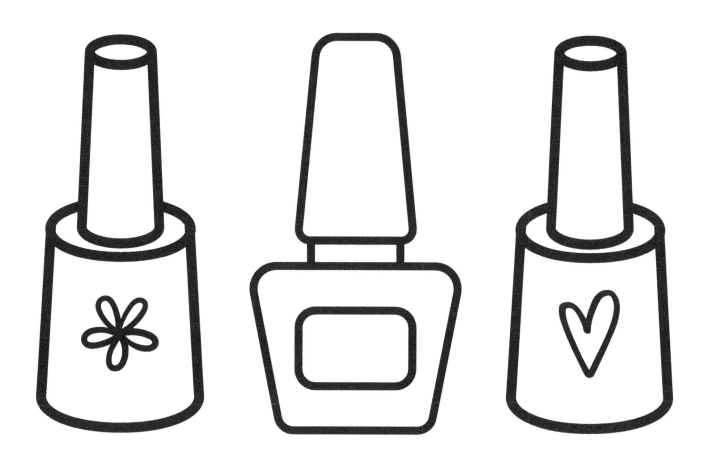

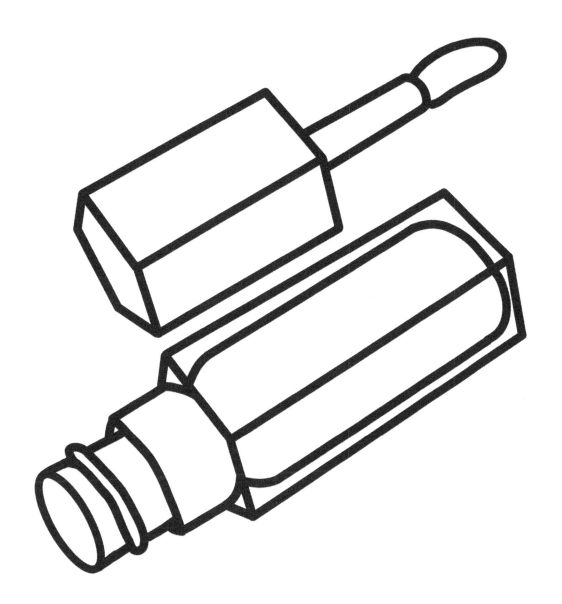

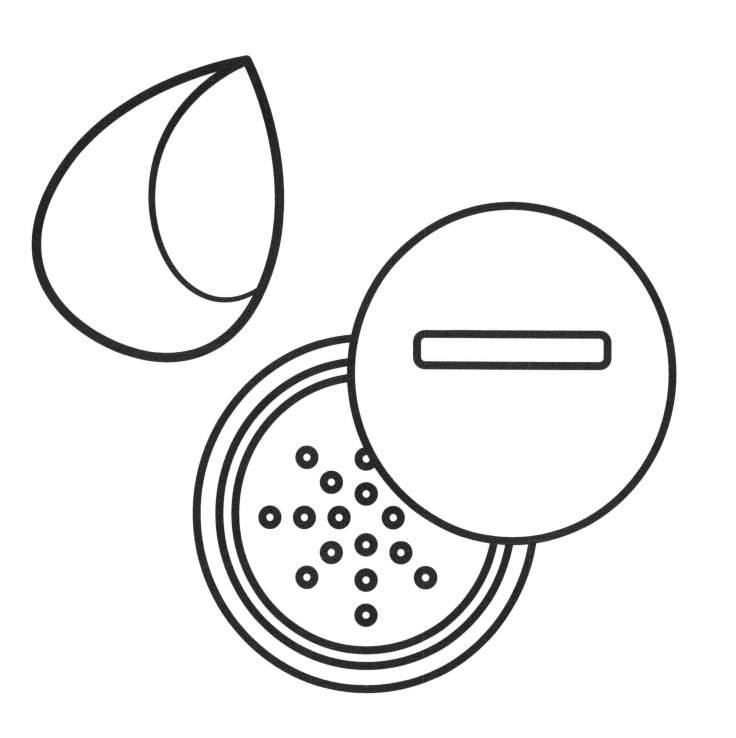

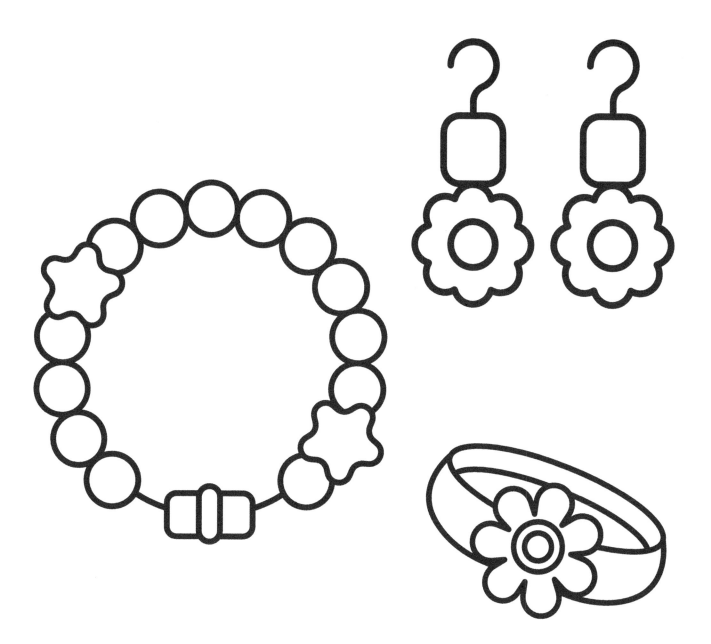

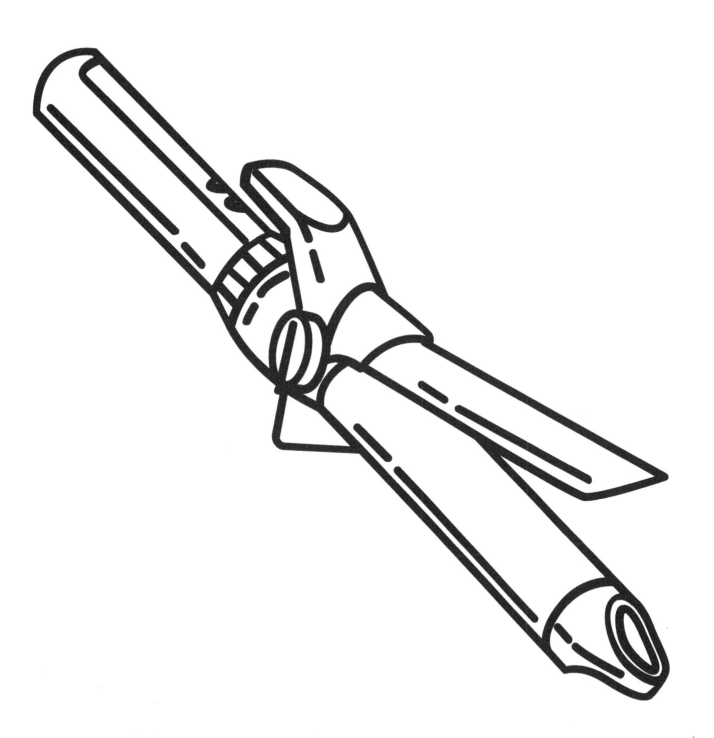

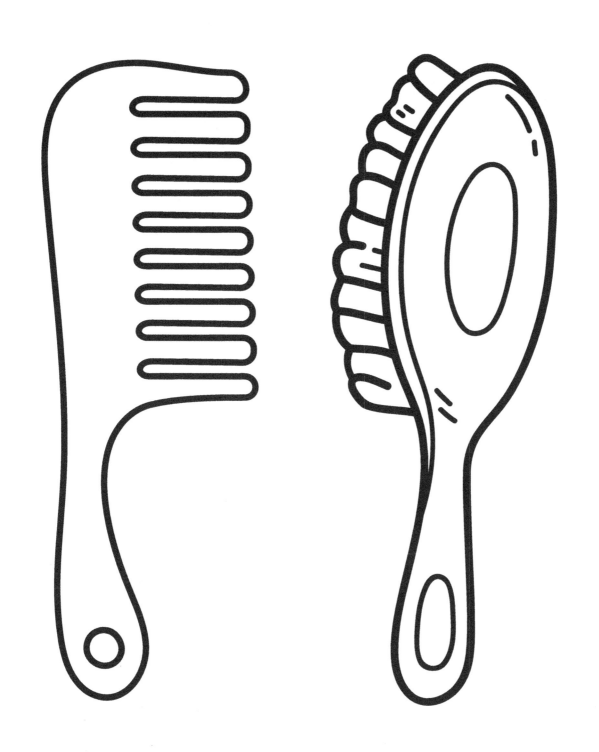

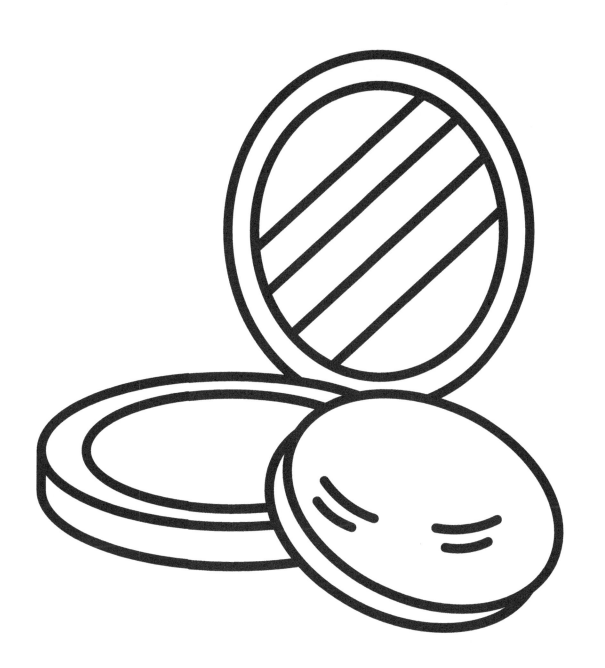

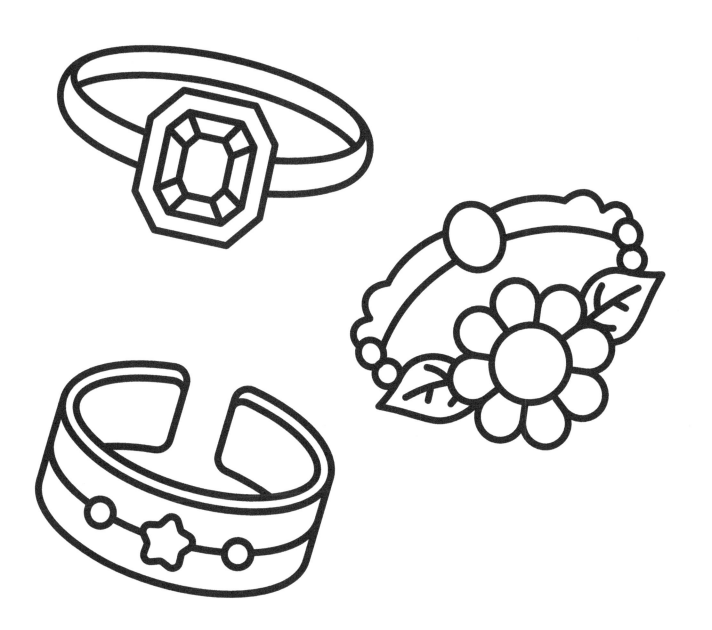

Made in United States
Orlando, FL
27 October 2024

53170847R00057